Light Matters More

A book of poetry

Jennifer Gurney

ISBN: 978-93-6354-464-2

First Edition: 2025
Rs. 200/-

Cyberwit.net
HIG 45 Kaushambi Kunj, Kalindipuram
Allahabad - 211011 (U.P.) India
http://www.cyberwit.net
Tel: +(91) 9415091004
E-mail: info@cyberwit.net

Printed at Repro India Limited.

Dedication

Light Matters More is dedicated to my dad, Bob Heitman, with all my love.

Previously published in Five Fleas 9-17-23

I would know Tom Wait's
voice anywhere ….
all gravel and grit

Previously published in Haiku Corner 9-28-23

by the river
my thoughts float
upstream

Previously published in Five Fleas 9-28-23

fell asleep
in the sky
lightness of being

Previously published in Fireflies' Light, Issue 28, October 2023

fireflies dance
in the incandescent
indigo night

Previously published in Five Fleas 10-3-23

that wheels-up moment–
when anything
is possible

Previously published in The Haiku Foundation 10-4-23

grief is a snowflake
silently falling on me
blanketing in loss

Previously published in Five Fleas 10-11-23

coming into focus—
my gaze adjusts forward
20-20 hindsight

Previously published in Wise Owl - The Daily Verse 10-11-23

frogs call
from lake's edge –
one-sided love songs

Previously published in Wise Owl - The Daily Verse 10-11-23

a moth sips
wild-flower nectar
from nature's happy hour

Previously published in Wise Owl - The Daily Verse 10-11-23

the moon is
a force of nature —
pulling us in

Previously published in Five Fleas 10-15-23

nothing is as
unnerving as the

smoke

detector

chirping

Previously published in Haiku Corner 10-18-23

darkness falls
too soon each day—
I am not ready

Previously published in Lothlorien 10-19-23

your voice sings
Happy Birthday to me
frozen on my phone forever
how lucky I wasn't home
when you first called that year

Previously published in Lothlorien 10-19-23

a lone train whistle
through the open window
late at night
came to something
moving forward

Previously published in Lothlorien 10-19-23

Dave Matthews
Stevie Ray Vaughn
BB King
Joe Bonamassa
my blues brothers

Previously published in Lothlorien 10-19-23

Chihuly
pulls you upward
in a color explosion
at the Bellagio
Vegas, Baby!

Previously published in Lothlorien 10-19-23

grant me patience to
see the good in all people
even when it's hard
especially when it's hard
that's when I need it the most

Previously published in Lothlorien 10-19-23

sometimes haiku is
not enough space to convey
all that is needed
two more lines are required
so a tanka is the form

Previously published in Lothlorien 10-19-23

the raindrops
cry my tears for me
of sadness for your loss
and empathy
for those closest to you

Previously published in Lothlorien 10-19-23

you taught me Scrabble
as a very young girl
we played together often
each time I've ever since
your memory plays a hand

Previously published in Lothlorien 10-19-23

fireflies flashing
in the inky black night as
we sweat in the heat
of unnecessary fire
lit for ambiance

Previously published in Lothlorien 10-19-23

I love a dark night
and the time to be
a stargazer

Previously published in Five Fleas 10-23-23

what lies
in the human heart—
silent truth

Previously published in Five Fleas 10-23-23

my favorite clothes—
the ones that
once held you

Previously published in Five Fleas 10-30-23

Tolstoy's War and Peace–
thirteen hundred ninety two
pages of advice

Previously published in Five Fleas 10-30-23

letting go of fear
I step out of
the plane

Previously published in Five Fleas 10-30-23

letting go of
those voices in my head
saying I can’t

Previously published in Take 5, Theme: Childhood Memories, November 2023

I doubt I'll ever
be able to hear Stardust
without remembering
you humming along
as I practiced piano

Previously published in Take 5, Theme: Childhood Memories, November 2023

at our first
neighborhood talent show
Susie and I sang –
raindrops keep falling
under a wet umbrella

Previously published in Take 5, Theme: Childhood Memories, November 2023

my fourth birthday –
the entire neighborhood came
balloons on the mailbox
picnic tables in the garage
best party of my life

Previously published in Take 5, Theme: Childhood Memories, November 2023

Grandma had
a plastic tablecloth
one side Happy Birthday
other side Merry Christmas –
child of the Depression

Previously published in Take 5, Theme: Childhood Memories, November 2023

party line
black and white television
rotary dial
calling time and temperature
hand-crank windows

Previously published in Kyoto Haiku for Peace November 2023

a bright prayer flag waves
gently in the summer breeze
every prayer is peace

Previously published in King River Press, Folk Ku 11-2-23

when I am still
I can hear your voice in my heart
whispering your love

Previously published in Five Fleas 11-5-23

gentle breeze blows
cold upon my neck–
stepping through a ghost

Previously published in Five Fleas 11-5-23

the trees are barren–
reminding me
of me

Previously published in Five Fleas 11-5-23

I long to spring forward
and yet I must
fall back

Previously published in Different Truths 11-8-23

lost in my thoughts
meandering through the day
time evaporates

Previously published in Different Truths 11-8-23

we reap
from the sacrifices
of those who came before

Previously published in Different Truths 11-8-23

letting go
of lifelong dreams is hard when
life has other plans

Previously published in Different Truths 11-8-23

time is
different
when traveling

Previously published in Different Truths 11-8-23

my cats always know
when I’m going on a trip–
suitcase is the tell

Previously published in Different Truths 11-8-23

on the cusp
of a new age
my heart is tender

Previously published in Different Truths 11-8-23

the power of
a single, shy
smile

Previously published in Different Truths 11-8-23

the melody plays
and I am transported through
time and space to you

Previously published in Different Truths 11-8-23

you have indelibly
written the poems of your love
on my heart forever

Previously published in Different Truths 11-8-23

sunlight dances
upon the page
illuminating words

Previously published in Enchanted Garden 11-11-23

a whole day
with my grown-up son –
best present ever

Previously published in Fresh Out Magazine 11-11-23

the half moon
plays jump rope
with the clouds

Previously published in Haiku corner 11-15-23

in the bittersweet
between autumn and winter–
light matters more

Previously published in haikuNetra 11-16-23

the weight of you
on my lap –
centering

Previously published in haikuNetra 11-16-23

yoga
with my fourth grade class –
balancing act

Previously published in Cold Moon Journal 11-18-23

heavy heads
bow toward earth
sunflowers

Previously published in Five Fleas 11-24-23

moon shadow cognitive dissonance

Previously published in Five Fleas 11-24-23

on the other side of sadness anger

Previously published in Under the Basho - Personal Best 11-26-23

Prior to that Previously published in Different Truths 8-10-23

interconnected
they pull on my heartstrings —
the moon, the waves

Previously published in The LEAF, Issue 2, December 2023

the feel of earth
beneath my feet
grounds me

Previously published in TAJ Mahal Review December 2023

reaping the harvest–
grandchildren
from children

Previously published in TAJ Mahal Review December 2023

there they go again—
raining down war
rattling the world

Previously published in TAJ Mahal Review December 2023

cherry picking
only
the best

Previously published in TAJ Mahal Review December 2023

I miss my mom today
nothing different today
just saying it outloud

Previously published in TAJ Mahal Review December 2023

worth thinking about:
the sound of children's laughter
the smell of spring rain

Previously published in TAJ Mahal Review December 2023

incessant dog –
even barks
in his sleep

Previously published in TAJ Mahal Review December 2023

one another's hearts
beating beside each other
love intertwined

Previously published in TAJ Mahal Review December 2023

I feel as if
I know the moon
as if it were a friend

Previously published in TAJ Mahal Review December 2023

purple
mountains
majesty

Previously published in TAJ Mahal Review December 2023

drips
of xylem sap
plant's own "dew"

Previously published in Five Fleas 12-3-23

no one to fill my stocking but myself I become Santa

Previously published in Five Fleas 12-3-23

Salvation Army shelter home for the holidays

Previously published in Cold Moon Journal 12-11-23

I hear your voice
each morning
in the birdsong

Previously published in Scarlet Dragonfly 12-12-23

whisperings–
voices unknown
and yet familiar

Previously published in Wise Owl - The Daily Verse 12-18-23

hope–
the first tulip through the snow
on a late winter day

Previously published in Wise Owl - The Daily Verse 12-18-23

thirty degree shift
in one day–
parka to flip flops

Previously published in Wise Owl - The Daily Verse 12-18-23

windswept patio
everything topsy-turvy
nature's spring cleaning

Previously published in Wise Owl - The Daily Verse 12-18-23

sweet peas exploding
on the river bank today–
fuchsia infusion

Previously published in First Literary Review-East January 2024

tree memory—
silently spoken
as we cross paths

Previously published in First Literary Review-East January 2024

a good day –
my work is done and
I'm empty of regret

Previously published in Scarlet Dragonfly 1-2-24

your love flickers
in a dark room
casting out sorrow

Previously published in Fresh Out Magazine 1-2-24

tasting like your lips
salty with tears
I enter the ocean

Previously published in Five Fleas 1-5-24

the new year dawns
before the sun rises—
damn-cat-knocks-phone-off-bedside-table-at-four-am

Previously published in Micropoetry Cosmos 1-6-24

that first snowflake–
magic as it melts
upon my tongue

Previously published in Micropoetry Cosmos 1-6-24

"ignight"
to light a fire at dark
to ward the cold

Previously published in Micropoetry Cosmos 1-6-24

when it's cold
I can always find you
by the space heater

Previously published in Micropoetry Cosmos 1-6-24

hard to get warm
when the cold is from
the inside

Previously published in Micropoetry Cosmos 1-6-24

the cold is lovely
soft and deep—
from my haven inside

Previously published in Micropoetry Cosmos 1-6-24

the cold stole
my beautiful golden tree—
with one big breath

Previously published in Micropoetry Cosmos 1-6-24

strange brew of laundry—
shorts from last weekend with
today's winter coat

Previously published in Micropoetry Cosmos 1-6-24

just a wink of winter
snow mixed with fallen leaves
before fall returns

Previously published in The Haiku Foundation 1-10-24

intermission–
a brownie helps
my heart unclench

Previously published in Five Fleas 1-13-24

is there anything
worse than an empty
fortune cookie

Previously published in The Rue Scribe 1-23-24

love descends like a
favorite down comforter —
a blanket for the heart

Previously published in The Rue Scribe 1-23-24

your frozen brilliance
stops me in my tracks—
moment of thanks

Previously published in The Rue Scribe 1-23-24

outlined in lace
your silhouette of ice—
frozen-framed

Previously published in The Rue Scribe 1-23-24

touched by
Mother Nature's
frosty fingertip

Previously published in The Rue Scribe 1-23-24

a lonely, soulful
saxophone
sends me

Previously published in Cold Moon Journal February 2024

sliver reflection–
a crack amidst the ice
where sky falls in

Previously published in 6th Basho-an International Haiku Contest - International Haiku Contest winner 2-10-24

I love that feeling—
your hand in mine
can't tell you from me

Previously published in Akitsu Quarterly Spring/Summer 2024

jumping off the dock
I joyfully cannonball
into summer

www.ingramcontent.com/pod-product-compliance
Ingram Content Group UK Ltd.
Pitfield, Milton Keynes, MK11 3LW, UK
UKHW041315190726
13845UKWH00025B/279

9 789363 544642